BODY BUTTER!

DIY BODY BUTTER GUIDE AND AWESOME BODY BUTTER RECIPES

Table of Contents

Introduction

Anyone who has ever tried body butter knows the luscious, skin-softening properties it possesses. Unfortunately, commercial body butter typically comes along with a high price tag and chemical ingredients that you wouldn't want to place on your skin. For those interested in a better option, make your own homemade body butter! Taking the do-it-yourself approach allows you complete control over the ingredients while still fitting into even the tightest budget.

Chapter 1 – Basic Ingredients and Tools

Even though the basic ingredients vary from one recipe to another, there are generally two main ingredients needed: liquid vegetable oil – such as olive oil, almond oil and sunflower oil – and solid vegetable fats, such as shea butter, palm oil or coconut oil. With this in mind, you can create your own body butter recipe that is unique to your needs and desires.

Essential oils are another ingredient that is commonly used in body butters but isn't necessarily required so they can usually be omitted if you don't have any on hand. Keep in mind, however, that essential oils provide various positive health effects that you will be missing out on if not added to the body butter.

As with the ingredients, there are a few tools you should have on hand when making body butter. Double boiler, stirring utensil, mixer and container is usually needed for the process. However, you can improvise on some of the tools. For example, if you don't have access to a double boiler then a glass bowl place on top of a pot of boiling water will work in a pinch. You can also simply use a pot or saucepan, making sure to stir constantly so the ingredients don't burn.

Another tool commonly used in when making your own body butter is an ice bath. An ice bath is essentially when a smaller bowl – typically filled with the ingredients you want to cool – is placed inside a larger bowl that is filled with ice. If you don't want to deal with the hassle of creating an ice bath, you can simple place the smaller bowl inside a refrigerator to cool.

Chapter 2 – Storing the Body Butter

It is best to store homemade body butter in amber or cobalt glass jars that are airtight. Clear glass jars will also work if they are kept out of direct sunlight and away from direct heat. Placing the jars in direct sunlight promotes oxidations, which ruins the body butter.

Many times, homemade body butters will begin to warm and melt, causing them to lose their whipped-like consistency. There is no need to panic and toss the body butter out if this occurs. Simply place it back into the refrigerator and re whip until it develops the desired constancy once again.

Chapter 3 – Shelf Life of Body Butter

Since most homemade body butters don't contain a preservative, their shelf life is less than that of commercial body butters. However, trying to pinpoint the exact shelf life is difficult since each body butter recipe contains varying ingredients. A good general rule of thumb, however, is to keep the body butter unrefrigerated for up to 2 months. Placing the body butter in the fridge will increase its lifespan but causes it to become hard. Instead, keep the body butter in a cool room and use within 2 months.

Chapter 4 – Body Butter Recipes

Whipped Body Butter

Ingredients:

- ½ cup mango or cocoa butter
- ½ cup shea butter
- ½ cup coconut oil
- ½ cup light olive, jojoba or almond oil
- 10 to 30 drops of essential oil (optional)

Directions:

Step 1: Combine the butters and oils together in a double boiler.

Step 2: Place the double boiler over medium heat and stir the ingredients constantly until they are completely melted.

Sep 3: Remove the melted mixture from heat and let cool for several minutes.

Step 4: Place the mixture in the refrigerator to cool for about an hour or until it begins to harden but is still a bit soft.

Step 5: Remove the mixture from the fridge and whip with a hand mixer until fluffy, which is usually about 10 minutes or so.

Step 6: Place the mixture back into the fridge for 10 to 15 minutes to allow it to set.

Step 7: Transfer your homemade whipped body butter to a glass jar with a lid until ready to use.

White Chocolate Whipped Body Butter

Ingredients:

- 1 cup cocoa butter
- 1 cup coconut oil

Directions:

Step 1: Add the cocoa butter and coconut oil into a saucepan.

Step 2: Place the saucepan on the stove set on low to medium heat.

Step 3: Stir the butter and oil with a wooden spoon continuously until the two ingredients are completely melted.

Step 4: Transfer the melted mixture into a clean container. Place inside a refrigerator until it begins to firm and becomes hardened.

Step 5: Remove the hardened body butter from the refrigerator. Use a hand mixer to whip the butter into a fluffy and light consistency.

Step 6: Store the white chocolate whipped body butter in a cool place.

Wild Rose Body Butter

Ingredients:

- 7 ounces shea, avocado or mango butter
- 2 ounces sunflower oil
- ½ ounce rosehip seed oil
- 8 drops rose absolute
- 10 drops geranium rose essential oil
- ½ teaspoon rose clay
- 2 teaspoons tapioca starch

Directions:

Step 1: Add the butter to a clean mixing bowl. Use a hand mixer to mix the butter. Start with the lowest speed and gradually increase the speed until the butter has a fluffy and light consistency.

Step 2: Add the sunflower oil, rosehip oil, geranium rose essential oil, rose clay and rose absolute.

Step 3: Mix the added ingredients into the butter with the mixer. Start at the lowest speed, gradually increasing it until the butter is light and fluffy. When the consistency resembles buttercream frosting, stop mixing.

Step 4: Spoon the homemade body butter into jars and secure the cap tightly. This recipe should fill about eight 2-ounce sized jars.

Soothing Lavender and Mint Body Butter

Ingredients:

- ¼ cup extra virgin coconut oil
- 3.4 cup Grade A unrefined shea butter
- 2 tablespoons calendula petals, dried
- 2 tablespoons marshmallow root, dried and cut up
- 8 drops lavender essential oil
- 8 drops peppermint essential oil

Directions:

Step 1: Preheat the oven to 200-degrees.

Step 2: Melt the coconut oil and shea butter together on the stove over low heat in an oven-safe pan. Stir in the petals and marshmallow root.

Step 3: Turn the oven off and immediately place the mixture-filled, oven-safe pan inside the oven.

Step 4: Let the mixture steep inside the oven for at least four hours.

Step 5: Remove the pan from the oven. If the mixture has solidified, simply warm it up over low heat on the stove until it melts again.

Step 6: Strain the herbs out of the oil using cheesecloth or a mesh strainer. Dispose of the herbs and place the oil in a mixing bowl.

Step 7: Place the oil-filled mixing bowl into the refrigerator until it becomes firm not solid. This typically takes a few hours.

Step 8: When the oil is firm, remove it the mixing bowl from the fridge and whip the oil with a hand mixer for about 30seconds.

Step 9: Use a spatula to scrape the sides and bottom of the bowl when the body butter starts to stick so you can thoroughly whip all the butter with the mixer.

Step 10: Add the essential oils to the body butter.

Step 11: Use the hand mixer to whip the essential oils into the body butter.

Step 12: Continue to whip the body butter until it starts to turn while and peaks form.

Step 13: Store the body butter in an airtight container until ready to use.

Mint Chocolate Body Butter

Ingredients:

- ½ cup cocoa butter, grated
- ½ cup shea or mango butter
- ½ cup coconut oil
- ½ cup mild olive or jojoba oil
- 1 to 2 teaspoons peppermint essential oil
- 2 tablespoons pure cocoa powder (if you want a version that isn't a bronzer and is more "white chocolate", use non-GMO cornstarch or arrowroot powder instead.)
- 2 teaspoons vitamin E (optional)

Directions:

Step 1: Place a small bowl – that can hold at least 5 cups of liquid -- in the middle of a larger bowl. Fill the larger bowl with ice.

Step 2: In a double boiler, melt the butters over low simmering heat.

Step 3: Add the coconut oil and continue melting until the ingredients are liquefied.

Sep 4: Remove the mixture from the stove.

Step 5: Gradually add the cocoa powder to the olive or jojoba oil.

Step 6: Add the cocoa powder and oil mixture to the melted butter/oil mixture, stirring together until well mixed.

Step 7: Transfer the mixture to the small bowl surrounded by ice and resting in the middle of the larger bowl. Let the mixture cool for 10 minutes.

Step 8: Once the mixture has cooled, add the essential oil and Vitamin E (if desired) and stir for several seconds.

Step 9: Remove the small bowl from the larger ice-filled bowl.

Step 10: Use a mixer to whip the mixture on medium to high speeds until stiff peaks begin to form. If the mixture isn't thickening, place the small bowl back into the larger ice-filled bowl and continue whipping.

Step 11: When the mixture has the consistency similar to buttercream frosting, transfer to container and store until ready to use.

Magnesium Body Butter

Ingredients:

- ½ cup magnesium flakes
- 3 tablespoons boiling water
- ¼ cup coconut oil, unrefined
- 2 tablespoons beeswax pastilles
- 3 tablespoons shea butter

Directions:

Step 1: Mix the magnesium flakes and boiling water in a small container. Stir until the flakes are well dissolved. You should be left with a thick liquid. Set the container aside for the moment to cool.

Step 2: Fill a small pan with about 1 inch of water and place on the stove.

Step 3: Sit a quart-sized mason jar in the middle of the small pan on the stove.

Step 4: Add the oil, beeswax and shea butter into the mason jar.

Step 5: Turn the stove on medium heat and allow the ingredients to melt, stirring with a wooden spoon.

Step 6: Remove the mason jar from the pan when the ingredients have completely melted. Let it cool to room temperature.

Step 7: Pour the contents of the mason jar into a blender. Blend the ingredients on medium speed.

Step 8: Add the magnesium mixture one drop at a time into the blender while still continuously blending the ingredients. Continue in this manner until all of the magnesium mixture has been added.

Step 9: Place the blender jar into the refrigerator for about 15 minutes and then re-blend until the consistency is that of body butter.

Step 10: Store the magnesium body butter in a cool location for up to two months.

Mint Infused Coconut Body Butter

Ingredients:

- 2 tablespoons shea butter
- 1 tablespoon mint-infused coconut oil
- 1 tablespoon olive oil
- Rose petals, dried
- Rosemary, fresh
- 1 capsule Vitamin E
- 7 drops lime essential oil
- 7 drops lavender essential oil

Directions:

Step 1: Melt the shea butter and coconut oil together in a pan over low to medium heat. Stir consistently to prevent the butter and oil from burning.

Step 2: Add the vegetable oil, dried rose petals and fresh rosemary to the melted mixture. Stir together and then simmer on low for 20 minutes.

Step 3: Let the mixture cool for a few minutes and then strain the herbs from the liquid.

Step 4: Open the vitamin E capsule and dump the contents inside the cooled liquid. Add the essential oils.

Step 5: Use a hand mixer to whip the ingredients together. Continue whipping until the body butter develops the right consistency.

Step 6: Store the butter in an airtight container.

3-Ingredient Cocoa Body Butter

Ingredients:

- 1.75 ounces cocoa butter
- 1.75 ounces wheat germ oil
- ½ teaspoon vitamin E oil (optional)

Directions:

Step 1: Place the cocoa butter in a double boiler over medium heat and melt.

Step 2: Remove the melted butter from heat and allow to cool for a few minutes.

Step 3: Once cool, add the wheat germ oil and vitamin E to the cocoa butter, stirring thoroughly for several seconds.

Step 4: Place the mixture into a fridge for about 5 to 10 minutes.

Step 5: After the allotted time, remove the mixture from the fridge and whip the ingredients with a hand mixture until the mixture develops a creamy consistency.

Step 6: Transfer the homemade body butter into an airtight container until you are ready to use.

Coconut Oil and Honey Body Butter

Ingredients:

- 1 ½ cups coconut oil
- 3 tablespoons honey
- 2 tablespoons grapefruit zests (any other citrus zests can be used)

Directions:

Step 1: Combine the coconut oil, honey and zest in a mixing bowl.

Step 2: Whip the ingredients together with a hand mixer until the consistency is creamy and a bit fluffy.

Step 3: Scoop the mixture into an airtight container or glass jar.

Simple Mango Body Butter

Ingredients:

- 3.5 ounces mango butter
- 2 tablespoons coconut oil
- 1 tablespoon beeswax
- 4 tablespoons kukui nut oil
- 3 tablespoons distilled water

Directions:

Step 1: Use a double boiler to melt the mango butter, coconut oil and beeswax together.

Step 2: Remove the melted mixture from the heat and allow to cool for several minutes.

Step 3: Add the kukui nut oil and distilled water to the mixture and stir until well mixed.

Step 4: Use a hand mixer to whip the body butter into a creamy consistency.

Step 5: Scoop out the body butter and store in an airtight container.

Coconut and Mango Body Butter

Ingredients:

- 30 grams coconut oil
- 30 grams mango butter
- 20 grams shea butter
- 30 drops mango essential oil

Directions:

Step 1: Place the coconut oil and shea butter into a pan. Heat the two ingredients on low to medium until the melt and become a liquid.

Step 2: Add the mango butter and then stir the ingredients slowly with a wooden spoon.

Step 3: Turn off the heat and let the mixture cool for 10 to 20 minutes, but don't let is set completely.

Step 4: Add the mango essential oil to the mixture and stir once again with the wooden spoon.

Step 5: Use a hand mixer to whip the ingredients until they are light and fluffy.

Step 6: Store the body butter in an airtight container.

3-Ingredient Shea Body Butter

Ingredients:

- 2.5 ounces shea butter
- 1 ounce macadamia nut oil
- 10 drops grapefruit essential oil

Directions:

Step 1: Melt the shea butter in a double boiler. When completely melted, remove from heat and let cool for several minutes.

Step 2: Add the macadamia nut oil and grapefruit essential oil and stir for several seconds until well mixed.

Step 3: Place the mixture into the refrigerator for about 6 minutes.

Step 4: Remove the cooled mixture from the fridge and use a hand mixer to whip the ingredients into a creamy consistency.

Step 5: Place the body butter in a jar and store in an cool, dry location.

Extreme Moisturizing Body Butter for Dry and Damaged Skin

Ingredients:

- 3.5 ounces shea butter
- 2.5 ounces coconut oil
- 1.75 ounces cocoa butter
- 1.75 ounces mango butter
- 1.75 macadamia oil
- 1.25 ounces avocado oil
- 1.25 jojoba oil
- 1.25 almond oil

Directions:

Step 1: Melt the butters and the coconut oil together in a double boiler.

Step 2: Remove the mixture from the heat when the ingredients are completely melted. Allow to cool for several minutes.

Step 3: Add the macadamia oil, avocado oil, jojoba oil and almond oil to the melted mixture. Stir thoroughly with a wooden spoon.

Step 4: Place the mixture back into the fridge for about 8 minutes.

Step 5: Remove the mixture from the fridge and whip with a hand mixer until you achieve a creamy consistency.

Step 6: Transfer the body butter into an airtight container until ready to use.

Hand Softener Body Butter

Ingredients:

- 2.5 ounces illipe butter
- 1 ounce almond oil
- 10 drops of essential oil (optional)

Directions:

Step 1: In a double boiler, melt the illipe butter.

Step 2: Remove the melted butter from the heat and allow to cool for several minutes.

Step 3: Add the almond oil and essential oils to the melted butter and stir until all ingredients are well mixed.

Step 4: Place the mixture in the refrigerator for 4 minutes.

Step 5: Remove the mixture from the fridge and whip it into a creamy consistency with a hand mixer.

Step 6: Transfer the mixture into a container.

Step 7: Use as a hand softening mask by massage the body butter into your hands before bed and then wearing cotton gloves while sleeping.

Cocoa and Hemp Body Butter

Ingredients:

- 3 tablespoons coconut oil
- 1 tablespoon beeswax
- 1 tablespoon castor oil
- 1 tablespoon sunflower oil
- 1 tablespoon hemp seed oil
- 1 tablespoon honey
- 10 drops essential oil (optional)

Directions:

Step 1: In a double boiler, melt the coconut oil and beeswax.

Step 2: Remove the melted oil and wax from heat and let cool for a few minutes.

Step 3: Stir in the rest of the oils and the honey.

Step 4: Use a hand mixer to whip the ingredients until they develop a creamy consistency.

Step 5: Pour the body butter into the container you are storing it in.

Aloe, Coconut and Lavender Body Butter

Ingredients:

- 4 tablespoons coconut oil
- 1 ½ tablespoons olive oil
- 2 tablespoons beeswax
- 1 teaspoon honey
- 3 tablespoons aloe vera gel
- 2 teaspoons lanolin
- 10 drops lavender essential oil
- 1 vitamin E capsule

Directions:

Step 1: Heat the oils, beeswax and honey over medium heat in a double boiler.

Step 2: In a separate saucepan, heat the aloe over medium heat until melted.

Step 3: Add the melted aloe into the melted mixture in the double boiler. Stir thoroughly.

Step 4: Add the lanolin to the mixture and stir together.

Step 5: Once all the ingredients are melted, remove from heat.

Step 6: Break open the vitamin E capsule and dump its contents into the mixture.

Step 7: Add the essential oil.

Step 8: Use a hand mixer to whip the ingredients until they are smooth.

Step 9: Store in airtight glass jars.

Peppermint Tallow Whipped Body Butter

Ingredients:

- 1 cup shea butter
- ½ cup tallow
- ½ cup jojoba oil
- 1 teaspoon peppermint essential oil
- 2 teaspoons vitamin E oil

Directions:

Step 1: Slowly heat the shea butter and tallow until the two ingredients are melted.

Step 2: Remove the butter and tallow from heat. Add the jojoba oil and stir with a wooden spoon.

Step 3: Let the ingredients chill in an ice bath for about 5 minutes.

Step 4: Stir in the peppermint essential oil and vitamin E oil.

Step 5: let the mixture chill in the ice bath a bit longer until it is completely chilled.

Step 6: Whip the homemade body butter with a hand mixer until stiff peaks begin to form.

Step 7: Transfer the body butter into airtight glass jars. Store the jars out of direct sunlight.

Vanilla Bean Body Butter

Ingredients:

- 1 cup raw cocoa butter
- ½ cup sweet almond oil
- ½ cup coconut oil
- 1 vanilla bean

Directions:

Step 1: Melt the butter and coconut oil over low heat. Remove the mixture from heat and let cool for for about 30 minutes.

Step 2: Grind the vanilla bean in a food processor or coffee grinder.

Step 3: Mix the sweet almond oil and bits of vanilla bean into the butter and oil mixture.

Step 4: Chill the mixture in the fridge for about 20 minutes. You want the oils to begin to solidify without completely hardening.

Step 5: Use an electric mixture to whip the mixture into a butter-like consistency.

Step 6: Store the body butter in glass jars.

Information: This recipe makes about 3 cups of whipped body butter.

Anti-Bacterial Body Butter

Ingredients:

- ½ cup coconut oil
- 6 tablespoons cocoa butter
- 2 tablespoons jojoba oil
- Few drops of Progest E (optional)
- 15 to 20 drops tea tree oil

Directions:

Step 1: Place the cocoa butter in an oven-safe glass container. Place the container in an oven set on low temperature for several minutes until the cocoa butter melts but doesn't become too hot.

Step 2: Remove the container from the oven and add the coconut oil and jojoba oil Stir the ingredients together until well combined.

Step 3: Set the mixture on the kitchen counter where it won't be disturbed for several hours or overnight. You want the mixture to start to solidify.

Step 4: Whip the solidified mixture for 6 to 10 minutes with a hand mixture. Stop and scrape the mixture off the sides if necessary.

Step 5: Add the tea tree oil to the body butter and whip once again with the hand mixture.

Step 6: Store the antibacterial body butter until ready to use.

Key Lime Whipped Coconut Oil Body Butter

Ingredients:

- ½ cup coconut oil
- 1 tablespoon olive oil (macadamia nut oil or castor oil can be used instead)
- 2 tablespoons aloe vera gel
- 20 drops lemon essential oil
- 20 drops lime essential oil

Directions:

Step 1: Place all the ingredients together in a mixing bowl.

Step 2: Set an electric mixer with a wire whisk attachment on high and whip the ingredients together for 3 to 7 minutes until you achieve an airy, light consistency.

Step 3: Scoop the whipped body butter into airtight glass jars. Store the homemade body butter in a cool, dry place.

Whipped Peppermint Body Butter

Ingredients:

- ½ cup coconut oil
- ½ cup cocoa butter
- ½ cup shea butter
- ½ cup sweet almond oil
- 1 teaspoon vitamin E oil
- 2 to 4 drops peppermint essential oil

Directions:

Step 1: Fill a medium-sized pot with the coconut oil, cocoa butter and shea butter. Set the pot on the stove and melt under low heat making sure to stir constantly until the ingredients are completely melted.

Step 2: Remove the pot from the heat.

Step 3: Mix the sweet almond oil, vitamin E and peppermint essential oils into the melted ingredients.

Step 4: Allow the mixture to chill in the fridge for about an hour or two. The mixture will be ready when it is firm but not completely solidified.

Step 5: Whip the ingredients with a hand mixer or stand mixer until you achieve a whipped yet smooth consistency.

Step 6: Fill glass jars with the body butter and store at room temperature out of direct sunlight and away from direct heat.

Lavender Body Butter

Ingredients:

- 4 tablespoons coconut oil
- 1.5 tablespoons olive oil
- 2 tablespoons beeswax
- 1 teaspoon honey
- 3 tablespoons aloe vera gel
- 2 teaspoons lanolin
- 10 drops lavender essential oil
- 1 vitamin E capsule

Directions:

Step 1: Place a double boiler on medium heat. Add the oils, beeswax and honey to the double boiler and melt.

Step 2: Heat the aloe in a second double boiler until melted.

Step 3: Add the aloe to the oils, beeswax and honey. Stir thoroughly for several seconds.

Step 4: Add the lanolin and stir once again.

Step 5: Remove the mixture from the heat.

Step 6: Open the vitamin E capsule and pour the contents into the mixture.

Step 7: With a hand mixer, whip the contents until it achieves the consistency of body butter.

Step 8: Let the butter cool before storing it in airtight containers.

Rosemary Mint Body Butter

Ingredients:

- 45 grams cocoa butter
- 90 grams shea butter
- 45 grams kukui nut oil
- 20 drops spearmint essential oil
- 10 drops rosemary essential oil

Directions:

Step 1: Add the cocoa butter and shea butter into a glass dish.

Step 2: Drizzle the kukui nut oil over top the two butters.

Step 3: Set the glass bowl on top of a pan filled with simmering water.

Step 4: Let the ingredients melt over the simmering water. Stir constantly while the ingredients are melting.

Step 5: Remove the glass dish from heat and let cool to room temperature.

Step 6: Let the mixture cool for about 10 minutes before transferring it to the freezer to cool for an addition 20 minutes.

Step 7: Remove the mixture from the freezer. Whisk the mixture with a hand mixer for about 5 minutes before placing it back into the freezer for 15 to 20 minutes.

Step 8: Remove the mixture from the freezer yet again and whisk with the mixer until you achieve a fluffy, airy consistency. If necessary, return the mixture to the freezer for an addition 15 minutes before whisking again.

Step 9: Fill the airtight container with the body butter and place in a cool location until you are ready to use.

Coconut & Rose Body Butter

Ingredients:

- 60 grams coconut oil
- 10 grams jojoba oil
- 1 milliliter alkanet infused oil
- 3 grams cornstarch
- 10 drops rose essential oil

Directions:

Step 1: Place the coconut oil, jojoba oil, alkanet infused oil and cornstarch in a glass bowl.

Step 2: Place a pan filled with water on the stove and bring the water to a boil. Turn the heat down so the water stays at a simmer.

Step 3: Place the glass bowl filled with the first 4 ingredients on top of the pan filled with simmering water.

Step 4: Let the ingredients melt, mixing them all together with a whisk. Remove the mixture from the heat and let cool to room temperature.

Step 5: Add the essential oil to the mixture once it cools to room temperature.

Step 6: Whisk all the ingredients together until you achieve a light and fluffy consistency.

Step 7: Enjoy! Store the leftover body butter in an airtight glass jar.

Cinnamon Body Butter for Cellulite

Ingredients:

- 100 grams coconut oil
- 50 grams cocoa butter
- 50 grams shea butter
- 30 drops cinnamon oil
- Cinnamon Stick

Directions:

Step 1: Warm the cocoa butter and shea butter on the stove with low or medium heat. Stir constantly until the two ingredients have melted.

Step 2: Slowly add the coconut oil to the mixture and stir for about a minute.

Step 3: Remove the ingredients from the heat and let cool for 10 to 20 minutes.

Step 4: Once cooled, immediately add the cinnamon oil.

Step 5: Use a mixer to whip the ingredients into a fluffy, light consistency.

Step 6: Scoop the body butter into small glass, airtight jars.

Step 7: Break the cinnamon stick into small pieces. Stick a piece of the cinnamon stick into each jar of body butter.

Step 8: Secure the lid on the jars. Give the jars of homemade body butter to your friends and family! But don't forget to keep some for yourself!

Edible Chocolate Body Butter

Ingredients:

- ¾ cup coconut oil, melted
- 1/3 cup clear agave nectar
- ½ tablespoon vanilla powder
- ¼ cup cacao powder (add a bit more if you want a thicker texture)

Optional Ingredients

- ½ teaspoon cistanche (an herb that promotes sexual prowess)
- 1 teaspoon maca (known to balance hormones and strengthens libidos)
- 1 to 2 drops rose essential oil
- ½ teaspoon powdered lavender flowers

Directions:

Step 1: Add all the desired ingredients into a food processor.

Step 2: Blend the ingredients until they are well incorporated.

Step 3: Transfer the mixture into a glass jar.

Step 4: Store the mixture either in the fridge or in a cool room until ready to use.

Coffee Body Butter Foot Cream

Ingredients:

- 0.7 ounces white beeswax
- 3.1 ounce coffee butter
- 2.4 ounces sunflower oil
- 1.2 ounces stearic acid
- 1 ounce emulsifying wax
- 15.6 ounces distilled water
- 5 milliliters dark rick chocolate fragrance oil
- 5 milliliters peppermint 2nd distillation essential oil
- 0.2 ounce optiphen

Directions:

Step 1: Using a microwave, melt the emulsifying wax, beeswax, stearic acid, coffee butter and sunflower oil together in a heat-safe container.

Step 2: In a separate heat-safe container, heat the distilled water to around 150 to 155 degrees.

Step 3: The temperature of the oil mixture must be within 5 to 10 degrees of the water's temperature. If it is not, stick the oil mixture back into the microwave for a few seconds.

Step 4: Pour the oil mixture carefully into the water and blend continuously for 3 minutes.

Step 5: Add the optiphen, chocolate fragrance oil and peppermint essential oil to the mixture, stirring until well blended. The temperature of the mixture cannot be above 176 degrees when adding the preservative optiphen or it will render it ineffective. Keep this in mind when adding it to the mixture.

Step 6: Microwave the mixture once again for a few minutes until it is warm.

Step 7: Immediately pour the mixture into glass jars. Let the jars sit overnight before placing the lid on them.

Step 8: Use a spoon to whip the mixture up inside the jars. Secure the jar closed with its lid and place in a cool room.

Dreamy Lemon Cream Body Butter

Ingredients:

- 6 tablespoons coconut oil
- ¼ cup cacao butter
- 1 tablespoon vitamin E oil
- ¼ teaspoon lemon essential oil

Directions:

Step 1: Combine the coconut oil and cacao butter in a saucepan and melt over low heat.

Step 2: Remove the saucepan from heat. Add the essential oil and vitamin E oil, stirring with a spoon.

Step 3: Let the mixture cool for a few hours at room temperature.

Step 4: Transfer the body butter to an airtight container.

Super Glowy Body Butter

Ingredients:

- 2 cups organic coconut oil, extra virgin and raw
- 7 ounces shea butter
- 1 drop tea tree oil
- Essential oil of your choice (such as lavender, peppermint or jasmine)

Directions:

Step 1: Melt the coconut oil and shea butter together in a double boiler.

Step 2: Remove the mixture from heat.

Step 3: Mix the tea tree oil and essential oil to the mixture. Blend for about 1 minute.

Step 4: Allow the mixture to cool and begin to solidify. This will take several hours at room temperature. You can speed the process up by placing the mixture in the fridge.

Step 5: Once the mixture has solidified, whip it into a light and fluffy consistency with a hand mixer.

Step 6: Scoop the body butter into airtight glass jars.

Black Raspberry and Vanilla Body Butter

Ingredients:

- 156 grams cocoa butter
- 155 grams shea butter
- 24 grams grapeseed oil
- 65 grams apricot kernel oil
- 4 grams vitamin E oil
- 10 grams black raspberry vanilla fragrance oil

Directions:

Step 1: Melt the butters, grapeseed oil and apricot kernel oil together in a double boiler. Heat until the ingredients are completely melted and well mixed.

Step 2: Remove the mixture from the heat. Add the vitamin E oil and fragrance oil. Stir for several minutes.

Step 3: Transfer the mixture to a clean mixing bowl. Place the missing bowl inside a separate, larger bowl that is filled with ice.

Step 4: Let the mixture cool in the ice bath for 20 minutes.

Step 5: Remove the mixture from the ice bath. Use a hand mixer to whip the ingredients for several minutes. Place the mixture back into the ice bath for an additional 20 minutes.

Step 6: Repeat Step 5 until the mixture develops a consistency of whipped butter.

Step 8: Scoop the body butter into airtight containers until ready to use.

The Simplest Body Butter

Ingredients:

- 1 cup cocoa butter
- ½ cup coconut oil
- ½ cup sweet almond oil

Directions:

Step 1: Melt the butter and oil together in a double boiler or saucepan.

Step 2: Transfer the melted mixture to mixing bowl. Add the sweet almond oil and blend.

Step 3: Place the mixture in the freezer for about 20 minutes until it has become solid but not hard.

Step 4: Use an electric whisk to whip the mixture into a fluffy white cloud.

Step 5: Spoon the mixture into a clean container until ready to slather it on.

The Wonderful Body Butter Recipe

Ingredients:

- 1 cup organic coconut oil
- 1 teaspoon vitamin E oil
- 3 drops pure vanilla essential oil

Directions:

Step 1: Place all the ingredients in a large mixing bowl.

Step 2: Use an electric mixer to whip the ingredients into a fluffy, soft consistency.

Step 3: Transfer the body butter to several small jars or one larger airtight glass container.

Sacred Frankincense Body Butter

Ingredients:

- ½ cup coconut oil, virgin and organic
- ½ cup shea butter
- ½ cup mango butter
- 1 ounce cocoa butter, raw and organic
- 1 teaspoon vitamin E oil
- 30 drops sacred frankincense essential oil

Directions:

Step 1: Combine the shea butter, mango butter and cocoa butter together in a double boiler. Let the three ingredients melt.

Step 2: Pour the melted butters into a clean mixing bowl.

Step 3: Stir the coconut oil into the melted butters.

Step 4: Let the mixture cool on the counter top for about 45 minutes.

Step 5: Stir the vitamin E oil and frankincense essential oil into the mixture.

Step 6: Cover the mixing bowl and place inside the fridge for about 40 minutes. You want the mixture to begin to solidify but not become too hard.

Step 7: Whip the mixture with a hand mixer until fluffy peaks form.

Step 8: Scoop the body butter into mason jars and store in a cool location.

Ultra Moisturizing Body Butter

Ingredients:

- ½ cup shea butter
- ½ cup mango butter
- ½ cup coconut oil
- ½ cup liquid oil, such as almond, sunflower, olive or grapeseed
- 2 tablespoon arrowroot powder
- 1 teaspoon vitamin E oil

Directions:

Step 1: Melt the butters and coconut oil together in a double boiler.

Step 2: Remove the mixture from the heat and let cool for about 20 minutes.

Step 3: Place the cooled mixture into an ice bath.

Step 4: While the mixture is cooling in an ice bath, mix the liquid oil, vitamin E oil and arrowroot powder together in a separate bowl.

Step 5: When the mixture in the ice bath begins to harden with a small pool of liquid on the top, add the oil/arrowroot concoction and whisk with a hand mixer.

Step 6: Continue whisking until it develops the consistency of creamy whipped butter. If the mixture isn't solid enough to whip, return it to the ice bath for an additional 20 minutes.

Step 7: Transfer the body butter to an airtight container to store until needed.

Scrumptious Body Butter

Ingredients:

- 3 ounces shea butter
- 2 ounces mango butter
- 1ounce coconut oil
- 3 ounces grapeseed oil
- ½ ounce beeswax
- 2 ounces distilled water
- 2 ounces aloe vera gel
- Essential oils of your choice (optional)

Directions:

Step 1: Melt the butters, oils and wax together in a double boiler, stirring occasionally.

Step 2: Once melted, pour the mixture into a blender and let cool.

Step 3: Pour the distilled water and aloe vera gel in a small bowl and let come to room temperature.

Step 4: When the butter, oil and wax mixture has cooled completely, turn on the blender and slowly add the water and aloe vera gel. If necessary, scrape down the sides of the blender.

Step 5: Once completely blended, add your desired essential oils and continue to blend. Skip this step if you are not using essential oils.

Step 6: Once the body butter achieves the desired consistency, transfer to glass jars. The body butter can be stored at room temperature in a cool room or in a fridge.

Shea and Coconut Body Butter

Ingredients:

- ½ cup shea butter
- ¼ cup coconut oil
- ¼ cup almond or olive oil
- 10 to 15 drops essential oil

Directions:

Step 1: Mix all the ingredients together in a double boiler and melt over medium heat.

Step 2: Once the ingredients are melted and well blended, pour into a mixing bowl and let cool in a fridge for about 30 to 60 minutes.

Step 3: Remove the bowl from the fridge.

Step 4: Whip the mixture with a hand mixer for about 10 minutes, or until the mixture begins to resemble whipped cream.

Step 5: Scoop the body butter into a storage jar.

Sugar Cookie Body Butter

Ingredients:

- 100 grams cocoa butter
- 100 grams mango butter
- 100 grams shea butter
- 48 grams argan oil
- 52 grams fractionated coconut oil
- 4 grams vitamin E oil
- 10 grams sugar cookie fragrance oil

Directions:

Step 1: Melt the butters, argan oil and coconut oil together in a double boiler, stirring continuously.

Step 2: Remove the melted mixture from heat and add the vitamin E and sugar cookie fragrance oil. Stir the ingredients together with a stainless steel spoon.

Step 3: Transfer the mixture into a clean mixing bowl. Place the bowl in an ice bath or set inside the fridge to cool. The mixture will become thicker as it cools.

Step 4: Every 20 minutes, use a hand mixer to whip the body butter for several minutes before returning it to the ice bath or fridge.

Step 5: Repeat Step 4 until the mixture resembles whipped butter.

Step 6: Spoon the mixture into the jars and enjoy!

Honey Kissed Body Butter

Ingredients:

- ¾ cup cocoa butter
- ¾ cup shea butter
- 2 tablespoons jojoba or apricot kernel oil
- ¼ teaspoon vitamin E oil
- 1 tablespoon honey powder

Directions:

Step 1: Melt the cocoa and shea butter together in a double boiler.

Step 2: Remove the mixture from heat and stir in the remaining ingredients with a metal spoon.

Step 3: Let the mixture sit out on your kitchen counter for several hours to cool.

Step 4: Use a hand mixer to whip the mixture until it resembles whipped cream.

Step 5: Store the mixture in an airtight container.

Sparkling Citrus Mango Body Butter

Ingredients:

- 2/3 cup shea butter
- 1/3 cup mango butter
- 1 teaspoon jojoba oil
- 3 teaspoons grapeseed oil
- ¼ teaspoon vitamin E oil
- 10 drops bergamot essential oil
- 8 drops palmarose essential oil
- 8 drops lemongrass essential oil
- 2 drops cypress essential oil
- 1 drop rose geranium essential oil
- 1 teaspoon cornstarch
- Cosmetic mica (gives it a glittery appearance)

Directions:

Step 1: Melt the shea and mango butter together in a double boiler.

Step 2: Remove the melted butters from heat. Stir in the remaining ingredients.

Step 3: Let the body butter cool for several hours. To speed up the cooling process, sit the mixture inside the fridge.

Step 4: With a hand mixer, whip the mixture for several minutes until it develops the consistency similar to whipped cream. If necessary, return the mixture to the fridge to cool longer before continuing to whip.

Step 5: Use a metal spoon to scoop the mixture into glass jars. Store the body butter-filled jars in a cool location out of direct sunlight.

Lavender Spice Body Butter

Ingredients:

- 1/4 cup cocoa butter
- 1 cup shea butter
- 2 tablespoons Kukui or Sweet Almond oil
- 1 tablespoon jojoba oil
- 1 tablespoon rosehip oil
- 1/4 teaspoon vitamin E
- 1 teaspoon cornstarch
- 20 drops lavender essential oil
- 4 drops patchouli essential oil
- 4 drops sandalwood essential oil
- 2 drops cedarwood essential oil

Directions:

Step 1: In a double boiler, melt the cocoa and shea butter. Once completely melted, remove from heat.

Step 2: Add the remaining ingredients and stir with a metal spoon.

Step 3: Let the mixture sit for several hours until completely cooled and beginning to harden.

Step 4: Grab your hand mixer and whip the mixture until it has a consistency that is light and fluffy, similar to whipped cream.

Step 5: Spoon the mixture into small glass jars.

Lavender Flower Body Butter

Ingredients:

- 1/4 cup cocoa butter
- 1 cup shea butter
- 2 tablespoons Kukui or Sweet Almond oil
- 1 tablespoon jojoba oil
- 1 tablespoon rosehip oil
- 1/4 teaspoon vitamin E
- 1 teaspoon cornstarch
- 20 drops lavender essential oil
- 5 drops frankincense essential oil
- 2 drops palmarosa essential oil
- 2 drops rose germanium essential oil

Directions:

Step 1: In a double boiler, melt the cocoa and shea butter. Once completely melted, remove from heat.

Step 2: Add the remaining ingredients to the melted butters and stir with a metal spoon.

Step 3: Allow the mixture sit for several hours until completely cooled and beginning to harden.

Step 4: With a hand mixer, whip the mixture until it has a consistency that is light and fluffy. The body butter should have the consistency of whipped cream.

Step 5: Spoon the mixture into small glass jars and share with friends and family!

Body Butter To Die For

Ingredients:

- 2 tablespoons shea butter
- 1 tablespoon mint infused coconut oil
- 1 tablespoon olive oil
- Dried rose petals
- Fresh rosemary
- 1 vitamin E capsule
- 7 drops lime essential oil
- 7 drops lavender essential oil

Directions:

Step 1: Melt the shea butter and coconut oil together in a double boiler.

Step 2: Add the vegetable oil and stir with a metal spoon.

Step 3: Add the dried rose petals and fresh rosemary. Heat the mixture on low for about 20 minutes. Remove the mixture from heat.

Step 4: Strain the rose petals and rosemary from the liquid. Let the mixture cool until it reaches room temperature.

Step 5: Open the vitamin E capsule and dump the contents into the mixture. Add the essential oils and stir with a metal spoon.

Step 6: Whip the mixture for 5 to 10 minutes until it has a light and airy consistency. If the mixture isn't developing the right consistency, place it in the fridge to cool for a bit longer.

Step 7: Use a spatula to scoop the body butter into an airtight jar.

Manly Body Butter

Ingredients:

- ½ cup olive oil, extra virgin
- ¼ cup coconut oil, extra virgin
- ½ cup water
- 1 tablespoon vitamin E oil
- 1 tablespoon vitamin D oil
- 1 teaspoon tea tree oil
- 2 ounces beeswax

Directions:

Step 1: Combine the olive oil, coconut oil, water and beeswax in a small pot.

Step 2: Heat on low to medium until the ingredients are melted.

Step 3: Pour the melted mixture into a mixing bowl.

Step 4: Use an electric mixer to beat the mixture for several minutes.

Step 5: Add the vitamin E, vitamin D and tea tree oil to the mixture. Mix once again for several minutes.

Step 6: Place the mixture in the fridge for a couple of minutes before removing it and beating it once again for 3 to 4 minutes.

Step 7: Repeat Step 6 until the mixture has the consistency of whipped cream.

Step 8: Spoon the mixture into a glass jar and use when needed.

White Chocolate and Peppermint Body Butter

Ingredients:

- 1/4 cup cocoa butter
- 1/4 cup coconut oil, virgin or refined
- 1/8 cup avocado oil
- 1 teaspoon red raspberry seed oil
- 10-15 drops of peppermint essential oil

Directions:

Step 1: Melt the cocoa butter, coconut oil and avocado oil together in a double boiler. Use a whisk to gently stir the ingredients together while melting.

Step 2: Remove the mixture from heat and allow to cool for several minutes.

Step 3: Add the raspberry seed oil to the mixture and stir with the whisk until well incorporated.

Step 4: Place the mixture in the fridge for about an hour. You want the mixture to cool and the liquid to begin setting up, but still soft enough for you to whip.

Step 5: Remove the mixture from the fridge and add the peppermint essential oil.

Step 6: With a hand mixer, whip the body butter for several minutes until it resembles whipped cream.

Step 7: Transfer the mixture to glass storage jars.

Sweet Citrus and Vanilla Body Butter

Ingredients:

- ¼ cup kokum butter
- ¼ cup coconut oil, virgin or refined
- 1/8 cup jojoba or avocado oil
- 1 teaspoon red raspberry seed oil
- 25 to 30 drops vanilla essential oil
- 15 drops tangerine essential oil
- 15 drops sweet orange essential oil
- 10 drops lemon essential oil

Directions:

Step 1: In a double boiler, melt the kokum butter, coconut oil and jojoba or avocado oil. Use a whisk to gently stir the ingredients together while melting.

Step 2: Once the ingredients are melted but not too hot, remove the mixture from heat and allow to cool for a few minutes.

Step 3: Add the raspberry seed oil to the mixture and stir with the whisk until well incorporated.

Step 4: Place the mixture in the fridge for about an hour. You want the mixture to cool and the liquid to begin setting up, but still soft enough for you to whip.

Step 5: Remove the mixture from the fridge and add the vanilla, tangerine, orange and lemon essential oil. Mix together with a metal spoon.

Step 6: Use a hand mixer to whip the body butter until it resembles whipped cream. Transfer the mixture to glass storage jars.

Lavender and Vanilla Body Butter

Ingredients:

- ¼ cup mango butter
- ¼ cup coconut oil, virgin or refined
- 1/8 cup avocado oil
- 1 teaspoon red raspberry seed oil
- 15 to 20 drops lavender essential oil
- 25 to 30 drops vanilla essential oil
- 4 to 8 drops carrot seed essential oil

Directions:

Step 1: In a double boiler, melt the cocoa butter, coconut oil and avocado oil. Use a whisk to gently stir the ingredients together while melting.

Step 2: Once the ingredients are melted but not too hot, remove the mixture from heat and allow to cool for several minutes.

Step 3: Add the raspberry seed oil to the mixture and stir with the whisk until well incorporated.

Step 4: Place the mixture in the fridge for about an hour. You want the mixture to cool and the liquid to begin setting up, but still soft enough for you to whip.

Step 5: Remove the mixture from the fridge and add the lavender, vanilla and carrot seed essential oil.

Step 6: With a hand mixer, whip the body butter for several minutes until it resembles whipped cream.

Step 7: Transfer the mixture to glass storage jars.

2-Ingredient Coconut and Vanilla Body Butter

Ingredients:

- 16 ounces coconut oil
- Vanilla extract

Directions:

Step 1: Place the coconut oil into a mixing bowl.

Step 2: Set a stand or hand mixer on high and mix the coconut oil for about 2 to 4 minutes. Make sure to stop the mixer every so often and scrap the coconut oil stuck on the sides down.

Step 3: Add a cap full of vanilla extract to the oil and continue mixing for an additional 4 to 5 minutes. The mixture should have a fluffy consistency.

Step 4: Scoop the body butter out and into small glass jars.

Belly Butter for Pregnancy

Ingredients:

- 1/2 cup organic mango
- 1/4 cup organic shea butter
- 1/4 cup organic cocoa butter
- 1/2 cup organic coconut oil
- 1/4 cup avocado oil
- 1/4 cup rosehip seed oil
- 2 tablespoons arrowroot powder or organic cornstarch
- 1 teaspoon vitamin E oil
- 1 teaspoon neroli essential oil
- 1 teaspoon lavender essential oil
- 1/2 teaspoon frankincense essential oil

Directions:

Step 1: In a double boiler, melt the mango, shea and cocoa butter. Add the coconut oil and stir with a wire whisk.

Step 2: Remove the melted butter and oil mixture from the heat.

Step 3: In a separate bowl, mix the arrowroot and avocado oil, stirring until the powder is completely dissolved.

Step 4: Stir the arrowroot and oil mixture into the melted mixture. Add the rosehip seed oil and stir again.

Step 5: Transfer the mixture to a mixing bowl and let cool in the fridge for a few hours.

Step 6: Remove the mixing bowl from the fridge and add the essential oils and vitamin E oil.

Step 7: With a hand mixer, whip the mixture on medium to high speed until it resembles a light and fluffy whipped cream.

Step 8: Transfer the belly butter to airtight jars.

Step 9: When ready to use, rub a small amount of the butter into your belly to help restore moisture to your skin.

Body Butter for Eczema

Ingredients:

- 2.5 ounces raw organic cocoa butter, shaved
- 3.5 ounces unrefined raw organic shea butter
- 3 tablespoons organic apricot oil
- 1 teaspoon vanilla extract
- ½ teaspoon vegetable glycerin

Directions:

Step 1: Place the shaved cocoa butter in a double boiler and melt on low to medium heat.

Step 2: Place the shea butter into a food processor. Pulse the food processor a few times to warm and loosen up the shea butter.

Step 3: Drizzle the melted cocoa butter over the shea butter. Add the apricot oil, vanilla and glycerin.

Step 4: Blend all the ingredients in the food processor until the mixture has a creamy and velvety texture.

Step 5: Scoop the mixture out of the food processor and into airtight glass jars.

Coconut and Plum Body Butter

Ingredients:

- 2 ounces coconut cream oil, virgin and organic
- 2 ounces cocoa butter, ultra refined
- 1 ounce plum kernel oil
- 1/2 ounce carnauba wax
- 1 ½ teaspoons plum jojoba wax beads

Directions:

Step 1: Melt the cocoa butter, coconut oil and waxes together in a double boiler over medium heat.

Step 2: Once melted, add the plum kernel oil and stir with a metal spoon.

Step 3: Remove the mixture from heat and place in an ice bath.

Step 4: After several minutes, use an electric mixer to whip the body butter into a light and airy consistency.

Step 5: When the body butter reaches the correct consistency – resembling frosting or whipped cream – spoon it into airtight containers.

Body Butter Bars

Ingredients:

- 1 cup shea butter
- 1cup cocoa butter
- 1cup sweet almond oil
- 2 cups beeswax pellets
- ½ cup jojoba oil
- ½ cupvirgin coconut oil
- ¼ teaspoon rose absolute
- ¼ teaspoon cocoa absolute

Directions:

Step 1: In a double boiler, heat the shea butter, cocoa oil, almond oil and beeswax together until just melted.

Step 2: Remove from heat and let cool for 2 minutes.

Step 3: Add the jojoba oil, coconut oil, rose absolute and cocoa absolute to the mixture and stir with a metal spoon.

Step 4: Pour the mixture into soap molds or a baking pan.

Step 5: Let the body butter cool and harden before removing them from the molds and wrapping in plastic wrap or storing in an airtight container.

Chapter 5– Tips and Considerations

Homemade body butter makes a thoughtful and well-loved gift for any occasion. In fact, some brides-to-be are making their own unique body butter to hand out as favors at their wedding. If you decide to give the gift of homemade body butter, remember to dress it up a bit. For an impressive presentation, scoop the homemade body butter into a piping bag – typically used for icing cakes and cookies – and pipe the body butter neatly into the gift containers. If you don't have piping bags on hand, you can make one by snipping the tip of the corner off a baggie and using that as a makeshift piping bag. Also consider, printing out a custom label that can be achieved to the top of the jar's lid. These labels can be printed with various pictures or words to fit your needs. For example, you can print labels that merely say 'Merry Christmas'', or make them a bit more personalized with 'From Amanda's Kitchen'. Once the body butter is inside the jar, tie a cute ribbon around the jar to finalize the presentation.

If making the body butter for children, avoid certain essential oils – such as peppermint – and instead use something a bit more gentle like lavender essential oil, which is typically recommended for children.

Conclusion

When making homemade body butter, the most important thing to remember is to have fun! Experiment with the many different essential oils that you can add. The essential oil itself provides various health benefits that can improve your overall well-being. For example, lavender has both calming and anti-bacterial properties, while clove can clear nasal decongestion and rose can improve the look of your skin. Mix and match ingredients to create your very own recipe that you can pass down for generations to come.

Made in the USA
Middletown, DE
09 August 2015